WINE DOSSIER

Mako Publishing, Incorporated • Charlotte, NC

First Printing   November 1995
Editor   Shawn M. Preston
Typesetting   R. Sean Miller
Printing   Josten's Printing

Copyright©1995 by:

MAKO Publishing, Incorporated
PO Box 470033
Charlotte, NC 28247

Telephone: 800-567-MAKO
704-292-1168
Fax: 704-292-1546
http://www.makopub.com

ISBN - 0-9647874-0-7

Other titles from Mako Publishing:
Beer Dossier
Cigar Dossier
Golf Dossier

From The Wine Cellar of

Wine Connoisseurs,

This book is designed to be a personal record of your wine tastings, meals and special occasions/events. Wine taste should be judged by you, using your own rating system. The label then saved and notes recorded to better understand what your palate enjoys. As you may know, the accompanying meal will have an effect on the taste of the wine. That is why it is important to also record the meal eaten with the tasting. At the rear of the book are sections to put your favorite wines (a "cheat sheet" for gift giving family, friends or colleagues), cellar notes to manage your wine supply plus space to put your local wine merchant's information.

The art of label removal is a tricky one. Most fine restaurants will be courteous enough to either remove the label for you or allow you to take the bottle home. When you are removing the wine label, soak a dishcloth in warm water, place it on the bottle for about 10-15 minutes, then carefully begin to remove the label with a razor. You will want to begin at the bottom corner and work your way to the top on that side. Continue to slowly work your way toward the opposite side working the razor (holding it at a 45 degree angle from the bottle) from top to bottom. Once the label is removed, allow it to dry for approximately 15-20 minutes and then secure it in the Wine Dossier with a spray adhesive. While the label is drying would be the perfect opportunity to record your notes and rating about that particular wine.

Enjoy!

Shawn M. Preston

"Be no longer a drinker of water, but use a little wine for thy stomach's sake and thine often infirmities" – 1 Timothy 5:23

WINE CELLAR NOTES

Wine _____ Vintage _____
Source _____ Price _____
Date purchased _____ Quantity stored _____

Date opened	Quantity used	Balance

Wine _____ Vintage _____
Source _____ Price _____
Date purchased _____ Quantity stored _____

Date opened	Quantity used	Balance

Wine _____ Vintage _____
Source _____ Price _____
Date purchased _____ Quantity stored _____

Date opened	Quantity used	Balance

Wine _____ Vintage _____
Source _____ Price _____
Date purchased _____ Quantity stored _____

Date opened	Quantity used	Balance

WINE CELLAR NOTES

Wine _____ Vintage _____
Source _____ Price _____
Date purchased _____ Quantity stored _____

Date opened	Quantity used	Balance

Wine _____ Vintage _____
Source _____ Price _____
Date purchased _____ Quantity stored _____

Date opened	Quantity used	Balance

Wine _____ Vintage _____
Source _____ Price _____
Date purchased _____ Quantity stored _____

Date opened	Quantity used	Balance

Wine _____ Vintage _____
Source _____ Price _____
Date purchased _____ Quantity stored _____

Date opened	Quantity used	Balance

WINE CELLAR NOTES

Wine _____ Vintage _____
Source _____ Price _____
Date purchased _____ Quantity stored _____

Date opened	Quantity used	Balance
_____	_____	_____
_____	_____	_____
_____	_____	_____

Wine _____ Vintage _____
Source _____ Price _____
Date purchased _____ Quantity stored _____

Date opened	Quantity used	Balance
_____	_____	_____
_____	_____	_____
_____	_____	_____

Wine _____ Vintage _____
Source _____ Price _____
Date purchased _____ Quantity stored _____

Date opened	Quantity used	Balance
_____	_____	_____
_____	_____	_____
_____	_____	_____

Wine _____ Vintage _____
Source _____ Price _____
Date purchased _____ Quantity stored _____

Date opened	Quantity used	Balance
_____	_____	_____
_____	_____	_____
_____	_____	_____

WINE CELLAR NOTES

Wine _____ Vintage _____
Source _____ Price _____
Date purchased _____ Quantity stored _____

Date opened	Quantity used	Balance

Wine _____ Vintage _____
Source _____ Price _____
Date purchased _____ Quantity stored _____

Date opened	Quantity used	Balance

Wine _____ Vintage _____
Source _____ Price _____
Date purchased _____ Quantity stored _____

Date opened	Quantity used	Balance

Wine _____ Vintage _____
Source _____ Price _____
Date purchased _____ Quantity stored _____

Date opened	Quantity used	Balance

WINE CELLAR NOTES

Wine ———————————————— Vintage ——————
Source ———————————————— Price ——————
Date purchased ———————————————— Quantity stored ——————

Date opened	Quantity used	Balance

Wine ———————————————— Vintage ——————
Source ———————————————— Price ——————
Date purchased ———————————————— Quantity stored ——————

Date opened	Quantity used	Balance

Wine ———————————————— Vintage ——————
Source ———————————————— Price ——————
Date purchased ———————————————— Quantity stored ——————

Date opened	Quantity used	Balance

Wine ———————————————— Vintage ——————
Source ———————————————— Price ——————
Date purchased ———————————————— Quantity stored ——————

Date opened	Quantity used	Balance

WINE CELLAR NOTES

Wine _____ Vintage _____
Source _____ Price _____
Date purchased _____ Quantity stored _____

Date opened	Quantity used	Balance

Wine _____ Vintage _____
Source _____ Price _____
Date purchased _____ Quantity stored _____

Date opened	Quantity used	Balance

Wine _____ Vintage _____
Source _____ Price _____
Date purchased _____ Quantity stored _____

Date opened	Quantity used	Balance

Wine _____ Vintage _____
Source _____ Price _____
Date purchased _____ Quantity stored _____

Date opened	Quantity used	Balance

WINE CELLAR NOTES

Wine _____ Vintage _____
Source _____ Price _____
Date purchased _____ Quantity stored _____

Date opened	Quantity used	Balance

Wine _____ Vintage _____
Source _____ Price _____
Date purchased _____ Quantity stored _____

Date opened	Quantity used	Balance

Wine _____ Vintage _____
Source _____ Price _____
Date purchased _____ Quantity stored _____

Date opened	Quantity used	Balance

Wine _____ Vintage _____
Source _____ Price _____
Date purchased _____ Quantity stored _____

Date opened	Quantity used	Balance

WINE CELLAR NOTES

Wine _____ Vintage _____
Source _____ Price _____
Date purchased _____ Quantity stored _____

Date opened	Quantity used	Balance

Wine _____ Vintage _____
Source _____ Price _____
Date purchased _____ Quantity stored _____

Date opened	Quantity used	Balance

Wine _____ Vintage _____
Source _____ Price _____
Date purchased _____ Quantity stored _____

Date opened	Quantity used	Balance

Wine _____ Vintage _____
Source _____ Price _____
Date purchased _____ Quantity stored _____

Date opened	Quantity used	Balance

WINE CELLAR NOTES

Wine _____ Vintage _____
Source _____ Price _____
Date purchased _____ Quantity stored _____

Date opened	Quantity used	Balance

Wine _____ Vintage _____
Source _____ Price _____
Date purchased _____ Quantity stored _____

Date opened	Quantity used	Balance

Wine _____ Vintage _____
Source _____ Price _____
Date purchased _____ Quantity stored _____

Date opened	Quantity used	Balance

Wine _____ Vintage _____
Source _____ Price _____
Date purchased _____ Quantity stored _____

Date opened	Quantity used	Balance

WINE CELLAR NOTES

Wine _____ Vintage _____

Source _____ Price _____

Date purchased _____ Quantity stored _____

Date opened	Quantity used	Balance

Wine _____ Vintage _____

Source _____ Price _____

Date purchased _____ Quantity stored _____

Date opened	Quantity used	Balance

Wine _____ Vintage _____

Source _____ Price _____

Date purchased _____ Quantity stored _____

Date opened	Quantity used	Balance

Wine _____ Vintage _____

Source _____ Price _____

Date purchased _____ Quantity stored _____

Date opened	Quantity used	Balance

WINE CELLAR NOTES

Wine _____ Vintage _____
Source _____ Price _____
Date purchased _____ Quantity stored _____

Date opened	Quantity used	Balance

Wine _____ Vintage _____
Source _____ Price _____
Date purchased _____ Quantity stored _____

Date opened	Quantity used	Balance

Wine _____ Vintage _____
Source _____ Price _____
Date purchased _____ Quantity stored _____

Date opened	Quantity used	Balance

Wine _____ Vintage _____
Source _____ Price _____
Date purchased _____ Quantity stored _____

Date opened	Quantity used	Balance

WINE CELLAR NOTES

Wine _____ Vintage _____

Source _____ Price _____

Date purchased _____ Quantity stored _____

Date opened	Quantity used	Balance

Wine _____ Vintage _____

Source _____ Price _____

Date purchased _____ Quantity stored _____

Date opened	Quantity used	Balance

Wine _____ Vintage _____

Source _____ Price _____

Date purchased _____ Quantity stored _____

Date opened	Quantity used	Balance

Wine _____ Vintage _____

Source _____ Price _____

Date purchased _____ Quantity stored _____

Date opened	Quantity used	Balance

WINE CELLAR NOTES

Wine _____ Vintage _____

Source _____ Price _____

Date purchased _____ Quantity stored _____

Date opened	Quantity used	Balance

Wine _____ Vintage _____

Source _____ Price _____

Date purchased _____ Quantity stored _____

Date opened	Quantity used	Balance

Wine _____ Vintage _____

Source _____ Price _____

Date purchased _____ Quantity stored _____

Date opened	Quantity used	Balance

Wine _____ Vintage _____

Source _____ Price _____

Date purchased _____ Quantity stored _____

Date opened	Quantity used	Balance

Attach Label Here

Wine _____ Vintage _____

Source _____ Price _____

Where tasted _____ Date _____

Occasion _____

With whom _____

Meal _____

Appearance _____ Bouquet _____

Balance _____ Taste _____

Body _____ Rating _____

Notes and comments _____

_____

_____

_____

_____

Attach Label Here

Wine _____ Vintage _____

Source _____ Price _____

Where tasted _____ Date _____

Occasion _____

With whom _____

Meal _____

Appearance _____ Bouquet _____

Balance _____ Taste _____

Body _____ Rating _____

Notes and comments _____

_____

_____

_____

_____

Attach Label Here

Wine _____ Vintage _____

Source _____ Price _____

Where tasted _____ Date _____

Occasion _____

With whom _____

Meal _____

Appearance _____ Bouquet _____

Balance _____ Taste _____

Body _____ Rating _____

Notes and comments _____

_____

_____

_____

_____

Attach Label Here

Wine _____   Vintage _____

Source _____   Price _____

Where tasted _____   Date _____

Occasion _____

With whom _____

Meal _____

Appearance _____   Bouquet _____

Balance _____   Taste _____

Body _____   Rating _____

Notes and comments _____

_____

_____

_____

_____

Attach Label Here

Wine _____ Vintage _____

Source _____ Price _____

Where tasted _____ Date _____

Occasion _____

With whom _____

Meal _____

Appearance _____ Bouquet _____

Balance _____ Taste _____

Body _____ Rating _____

Notes and comments _____

_____

_____

_____

_____

Attach Label Here

Wine _____   Vintage _____

Source _____   Price _____

Where tasted _____   Date _____

Occasion _____

With whom _____

Meal _____

Appearance _____   Bouquet _____

Balance _____   Taste _____

Body _____   Rating _____

Notes and comments _____

_____

_____

_____

_____

_____

Attach Label Here

Wine _____ Vintage _____

Source _____ Price _____

Where tasted _____ Date _____

Occasion _____

With whom _____

Meal _____

Appearance _____ Bouquet _____

Balance _____ Taste _____

Body _____ Rating _____

Notes and comments _____

_____

_____

_____

_____

Attach Label Here

Wine _____ Vintage _____

Source _____ Price _____

Where tasted _____ Date _____

Occasion _____

With whom _____

Meal _____

Appearance _____ Bouquet _____

Balance _____ Taste _____

Body _____ Rating _____

Notes and comments _____

_____

_____

_____

_____

Attach Label Here

Wine _____ Vintage _____

Source _____ Price _____

Where tasted _____ Date _____

Occasion _____

With whom _____

Meal _____

Appearance _____ Bouquet _____

Balance _____ Taste _____

Body _____ Rating _____

Notes and comments _____

_____

_____

_____

_____

Attach Label Here

Wine _____   Vintage _____

Source _____   Price _____

Where tasted _____   Date _____

Occasion _____

With whom _____

Meal _____

Appearance _____   Bouquet _____

Balance _____   Taste _____

Body _____   Rating _____

Notes and comments _____

_____

_____

_____

_____

_____

Attach Label Here

Wine _____ Vintage _____

Source _____ Price _____

Where tasted _____ Date _____

Occasion _____

With whom _____

Meal _____

Appearance _____ Bouquet _____

Balance _____ Taste _____

Body _____ Rating _____

Notes and comments _____

_____

_____

_____

_____

Attach Label Here

Wine _____ Vintage _____

Source _____ Price _____

Where tasted _____ Date _____

Occasion _____

With whom _____

Meal _____

Appearance _____ Bouquet _____

Balance _____ Taste _____

Body _____ Rating _____

Notes and comments _____

_____

_____

_____

_____

Attach Label Here

Wine _____ Vintage _____

Source _____ Price _____

Where tasted _____ Date _____

Occasion _____

With whom _____

Meal _____

Appearance _____ Bouquet _____

Balance _____ Taste _____

Body _____ Rating _____

Notes and comments_____

_____

_____

_____

_____

Attach Label Here

Wine _____ Vintage _____

Source _____ Price _____

Where tasted _____ Date _____

Occasion _____

With whom _____

Meal _____

Appearance _____ Bouquet _____

Balance _____ Taste _____

Body _____ Rating _____

Notes and comments _____

_____

_____

_____

_____

Attach Label Here

Wine _____ Vintage _____

Source_____ Price _____

Where tasted_____ Date _____

Occasion_____

With whom_____

Meal_____

Appearance _____ Bouquet _____

Balance _____ Taste _____

Body _____ Rating _____

Notes and comments_____

_____

_____

_____

_____

Attach Label Here

Wine _____ Vintage _____

Source _____ Price _____

Where tasted _____ Date _____

Occasion _____

With whom _____

Meal _____

Appearance _____ Bouquet _____

Balance _____ Taste _____

Body _____ Rating _____

Notes and comments _____

_____

_____

_____

_____

Attach Label Here

Wine _____ Vintage _____

Source _____ Price _____

Where tasted _____ Date _____

Occasion _____

With whom _____

Meal _____

Appearance _____ Bouquet _____

Balance _____ Taste _____

Body _____ Rating _____

Notes and comments _____

_____

_____

_____

_____

Attach Label Here

Wine _____ Vintage _____

Source _____ Price _____

Where tasted _____ Date _____

Occasion _____

With whom _____

Meal _____

Appearance _____ Bouquet _____

Balance _____ Taste _____

Body _____ Rating _____

Notes and comments _____

_____

_____

_____

_____

Attach Label Here

Wine _____ Vintage _____
Source _____ Price _____
Where tasted _____ Date _____
Occasion _____
With whom _____
Meal _____
Appearance _____ Bouquet _____
Balance _____ Taste _____
Body _____ Rating _____
Notes and comments _____
_____
_____
_____
_____

Attach Label Here

Wine _____ Vintage _____

Source _____ Price _____

Where tasted _____ Date _____

Occasion _____

With whom _____

Meal _____

Appearance _____ Bouquet _____

Balance _____ Taste _____

Body _____ Rating _____

Notes and comments _____

_____

_____

_____

_____

Attach Label Here

Wine _____   Vintage _____

Source _____   Price _____

Where tasted _____   Date _____

Occasion _____

With whom _____

Meal _____

Appearance _____   Bouquet _____

Balance _____   Taste _____

Body _____   Rating _____

Notes and comments _____

_____

_____

_____

_____

Attach Label Here

Wine _____ Vintage _____

Source _____ Price _____

Where tasted _____ Date _____

Occasion _____

With whom _____

Meal _____

Appearance _____ Bouquet _____

Balance _____ Taste _____

Body _____ Rating _____

Notes and comments _____

_____

_____

_____

_____

Attach Label Here

Wine _____ Vintage _____

Source _____ Price _____

Where tasted _____ Date _____

Occasion _____

With whom _____

Meal _____

Appearance _____ Bouquet _____

Balance _____ Taste _____

Body _____ Rating _____

Notes and comments _____

_____

_____

_____

_____

Attach Label Here

Wine _____ Vintage _____

Source _____ Price _____

Where tasted _____ Date _____

Occasion _____

With whom _____

Meal _____

Appearance _____ Bouquet _____

Balance _____ Taste _____

Body _____ Rating _____

Notes and comments _____

_____

_____

_____

_____

Attach Label Here

Wine _____   Vintage _____

Source _____   Price _____

Where tasted _____   Date _____

Occasion _____

With whom _____

Meal _____

Appearance _____   Bouquet _____

Balance _____   Taste _____

Body _____   Rating _____

Notes and comments _____

_____

_____

_____

_____

Attach Label Here

Wine _____ Vintage _____

Source _____ Price _____

Where tasted _____ Date _____

Occasion _____

With whom _____

Meal _____

Appearance _____ Bouquet _____

Balance _____ Taste _____

Body _____ Rating _____

Notes and comments _____

_____

_____

_____

_____

Attach Label Here

Wine _____ Vintage _____

Source _____ Price _____

Where tasted _____ Date _____

Occasion _____

With whom _____

Meal _____

Appearance _____ Bouquet _____

Balance _____ Taste _____

Body _____ Rating _____

Notes and comments _____

_____

_____

_____

_____

Attach Label Here

Wine _____ Vintage _____

Source _____ Price _____

Where tasted _____ Date _____

Occasion _____

With whom _____

Meal _____

Appearance _____ Bouquet _____

Balance _____ Taste _____

Body _____ Rating _____

Notes and comments _____

_____

_____

_____

_____

Attach Label Here

Wine _____   Vintage _____
Source _____   Price _____
Where tasted _____   Date _____
Occasion _____
With whom _____
Meal _____
Appearance _____   Bouquet _____
Balance _____   Taste _____
Body _____   Rating _____
Notes and comments _____
_____
_____
_____
_____

Attach Label Here

Wine _____ Vintage _____

Source _____ Price _____

Where tasted _____ Date _____

Occasion _____

With whom _____

Meal _____

Appearance _____ Bouquet _____

Balance _____ Taste _____

Body _____ Rating _____

Notes and comments _____

_____

_____

_____

_____

Attach Label Here

Wine _____   Vintage _____

Source _____   Price _____

Where tasted _____   Date _____

Occasion _____

With whom _____

Meal _____

Appearance _____   Bouquet _____

Balance _____   Taste _____

Body _____   Rating _____

Notes and comments _____

_____

_____

_____

_____

Attach Label Here

Wine _____ Vintage _____

Source _____ Price _____

Where tasted _____ Date _____

Occasion _____

With whom _____

Meal _____

Appearance _____ Bouquet _____

Balance _____ Taste _____

Body _____ Rating _____

Notes and comments _____

_____

_____

_____

_____

Attach Label Here

Wine _____ Vintage _____

Source _____ Price _____

Where tasted _____ Date _____

Occasion _____

With whom _____

Meal _____

Appearance _____ Bouquet _____

Balance _____ Taste _____

Body _____ Rating _____

Notes and comments _____

_____

_____

_____

_____

Attach Label Here

Wine _____ Vintage _____

Source _____ Price _____

Where tasted _____ Date _____

Occasion _____

With whom _____

Meal _____

Appearance _____ Bouquet _____

Balance _____ Taste _____

Body _____ Rating _____

Notes and comments _____

_____

_____

_____

_____

_____

Attach Label Here

Wine _____   Vintage _____

Source _____   Price _____

Where tasted _____   Date _____

Occasion _____

With whom _____

Meal _____

Appearance _____   Bouquet _____

Balance _____   Taste _____

Body _____   Rating _____

Notes and comments _____

_____

_____

_____

_____

Attach Label Here

Wine _____ Vintage _____

Source _____ Price _____

Where tasted _____ Date _____

Occasion _____

With whom _____

Meal _____

Appearance _____ Bouquet _____

Balance _____ Taste _____

Body _____ Rating _____

Notes and comments _____

_____

_____

_____

_____

Attach Label Here

Wine _____ Vintage _____

Source _____ Price _____

Where tasted _____ Date _____

Occasion _____

With whom _____

Meal _____

Appearance _____ Bouquet _____

Balance _____ Taste _____

Body _____ Rating _____

Notes and comments _____

_____

_____

_____

_____

Attach Label Here

Wine _____ Vintage _____

Source _____ Price _____

Where tasted _____ Date _____

Occasion _____

With whom _____

Meal _____

Appearance _____ Bouquet _____

Balance _____ Taste _____

Body _____ Rating _____

Notes and comments _____

_____

_____

_____

_____

Attach Label Here

Wine _____ Vintage _____

Source _____ Price _____

Where tasted _____ Date _____

Occasion _____

With whom _____

Meal _____

Appearance _____ Bouquet _____

Balance _____ Taste _____

Body _____ Rating _____

Notes and comments _____

_____

_____

_____

_____

Attach Label Here

Wine _____ Vintage _____

Source _____ Price _____

Where tasted _____ Date _____

Occasion _____

With whom _____

Meal _____

Appearance _____ Bouquet _____

Balance _____ Taste _____

Body _____ Rating _____

Notes and comments _____
_____
_____
_____
_____
_____

Attach Label Here

Wine _____ Vintage _____

Source _____ Price _____

Where tasted _____ Date _____

Occasion _____

With whom _____

Meal _____

Appearance _____ Bouquet _____

Balance _____ Taste _____

Body _____ Rating _____

Notes and comments _____

_____

_____

_____

_____

Attach Label Here

Wine _____ Vintage _____

Source _____ Price _____

Where tasted _____ Date _____

Occasion _____

With whom _____

Meal _____

Appearance _____ Bouquet _____

Balance _____ Taste _____

Body _____ Rating _____

Notes and comments _____

_____

_____

_____

_____

Attach Label Here

Wine _____	Vintage _____
Source _____	Price _____
Where tasted _____	Date _____
Occasion _____
With whom _____
Meal _____
Appearance _____	Bouquet _____
Balance _____	Taste _____
Body _____	Rating _____
Notes and comments _____

_____

_____

_____

_____

Attach Label Here

Wine _____ Vintage _____

Source _____ Price _____

Where tasted _____ Date _____

Occasion _____

With whom _____

Meal _____

Appearance _____ Bouquet _____

Balance _____ Taste _____

Body _____ Rating _____

Notes and comments _____
_____
_____
_____
_____

Attach Label Here

Wine _____	Vintage _____
Source _____	Price _____
Where tasted _____	Date _____
Occasion _____	
With whom _____	
Meal _____	
Appearance _____	Bouquet _____
Balance _____	Taste _____
Body _____	Rating _____

Notes and comments _____
_____
_____
_____
_____
_____

Attach Label Here

Wine _____   Vintage _____

Source _____   Price _____

Where tasted _____   Date _____

Occasion _____

With whom _____

Meal _____

Appearance _____   Bouquet _____

Balance _____   Taste _____

Body _____   Rating _____

Notes and comments _____

_____

_____

_____

_____

Attach Label Here

Wine _____ Vintage _____

Source _____ Price _____

Where tasted _____ Date _____

Occasion _____

With whom _____

Meal _____

Appearance _____ Bouquet _____

Balance _____ Taste _____

Body _____ Rating _____

Notes and comments _____

_____

_____

_____

_____

Attach Label Here

Wine _____ Vintage _____

Source _____ Price _____

Where tasted _____ Date _____

Occasion _____

With whom _____

Meal _____

Appearance _____ Bouquet _____

Balance _____ Taste _____

Body _____ Rating _____

Notes and comments _____

_____

_____

_____

_____

Attach Label Here

Wine _____ Vintage _____

Source _____ Price _____

Where tasted _____ Date _____

Occasion _____

With whom _____

Meal _____

Appearance _____ Bouquet _____

Balance _____ Taste _____

Body _____ Rating _____

Notes and comments _____

_____

_____

_____

_____

Attach Label Here

Wine _____ Vintage _____

Source _____ Price _____

Where tasted _____ Date _____

Occasion _____

With whom _____

Meal _____

Appearance _____ Bouquet _____

Balance _____ Taste _____

Body _____ Rating _____

Notes and comments _____
_____
_____
_____
_____

Attach Label Here

Wine _____   Vintage _____

Source _____   Price _____

Where tasted _____   Date _____

Occasion _____

With whom _____

Meal _____

Appearance _____   Bouquet _____

Balance _____   Taste _____

Body _____   Rating _____

Notes and comments _____

_____

_____

_____

_____

Attach Label Here

Wine _____ Vintage _____

Source _____ Price _____

Where tasted _____ Date _____

Occasion _____

With whom _____

Meal _____

Appearance _____ Bouquet _____

Balance _____ Taste _____

Body _____ Rating _____

Notes and comments _____

_____

_____

_____

_____

Attach Label Here

Wine _____	Vintage _____
Source _____	Price _____
Where tasted _____	Date _____
Occasion _____	
With whom _____	
Meal _____	
Appearance _____	Bouquet _____
Balance _____	Taste _____
Body _____	Rating _____

Notes and comments _____
_____
_____
_____
_____
_____

Attach Label Here

Wine _____ Vintage _____

Source _____ Price _____

Where tasted _____ Date _____

Occasion _____

With whom _____

Meal _____

Appearance _____ Bouquet _____

Balance _____ Taste _____

Body _____ Rating _____

Notes and comments _____

_____

_____

_____

_____

Attach Label Here

Wine _____   Vintage _____

Source_____   Price _____

Where tasted_____   Date _____

Occasion_____

With whom _____

Meal _____

Appearance _____   Bouquet _____

Balance _____   Taste _____

Body _____   Rating _____

Notes and comments_____

_____

_____

_____

_____

Attach Label Here

Wine _____ Vintage _____

Source _____ Price _____

Where tasted _____ Date _____

Occasion _____

With whom _____

Meal _____

Appearance _____ Bouquet _____

Balance _____ Taste _____

Body _____ Rating _____

Notes and comments _____

_____

_____

_____

_____

Attach Label Here

Wine _____ Vintage _____

Source _____ Price _____

Where tasted _____ Date _____

Occasion _____

With whom _____

Meal _____

Appearance _____ Bouquet _____

Balance _____ Taste _____

Body _____ Rating _____

Notes and comments _____

_____

_____

_____

_____

Attach Label Here

Wine _____   Vintage _____

Source _____   Price _____

Where tasted _____   Date _____

Occasion _____

With whom _____

Meal _____

Appearance _____   Bouquet _____

Balance _____   Taste _____

Body _____   Rating _____

Notes and comments _____

_____

_____

_____

_____

Attach Label Here

Wine _____	Vintage _____
Source _____	Price _____
Where tasted _____	Date _____
Occasion _____	
With whom _____	
Meal _____	
Appearance _____	Bouquet _____
Balance _____	Taste _____
Body _____	Rating _____
Notes and comments _____	

_____

_____

_____

_____

Attach Label Here

Wine _____ Vintage _____

Source _____ Price _____

Where tasted _____ Date _____

Occasion _____

With whom _____

Meal _____

Appearance _____ Bouquet _____

Balance _____ Taste _____

Body _____ Rating _____

Notes and comments _____

_____

_____

_____

_____

Attach Label Here

Wine _____ Vintage _____

Source _____ Price _____

Where tasted _____ Date _____

Occasion _____

With whom _____

Meal _____

Appearance _____ Bouquet _____

Balance _____ Taste _____

Body _____ Rating _____

Notes and comments _____

_____

_____

_____

_____

Attach Label Here

Wine _____ Vintage _____

Source _____ Price _____

Where tasted _____ Date _____

Occasion _____

With whom _____

Meal _____

Appearance _____ Bouquet _____

Balance _____ Taste _____

Body _____ Rating _____

Notes and comments _____

_____

_____

_____

_____

Attach Label Here

Wine _____   Vintage _____

Source _____   Price _____

Where tasted _____   Date _____

Occasion _____

With whom _____

Meal _____

Appearance _____   Bouquet _____

Balance _____   Taste _____

Body _____   Rating _____

Notes and comments _____

_____

_____

_____

_____

Attach Label Here

Wine _____ Vintage _____

Source_____ Price _____

Where tasted_____ Date _____

Occasion _____

With whom _____

Meal _____

Appearance _____ Bouquet _____

Balance _____ Taste _____

Body _____ Rating _____

Notes and comments_____

_____

_____

_____

_____

Attach Label Here

Wine _____ Vintage _____

Source _____ Price _____

Where tasted _____ Date _____

Occasion _____

With whom _____

Meal _____

Appearance _____ Bouquet _____

Balance _____ Taste _____

Body _____ Rating _____

Notes and comments _____

_____

_____

_____

_____

Attach Label Here

Wine _____ Vintage _____

Source _____ Price _____

Where tasted _____ Date _____

Occasion _____

With whom _____

Meal _____

Appearance _____ Bouquet _____

Balance _____ Taste _____

Body _____ Rating _____

Notes and comments _____

_____

_____

_____

_____

Attach Label Here

Wine _____   Vintage _____

Source _____   Price _____

Where tasted _____   Date _____

Occasion _____

With whom _____

Meal _____

Appearance _____   Bouquet _____

Balance _____   Taste _____

Body _____   Rating _____

Notes and comments _____

_____

_____

_____

_____

Attach Label Here

Wine _____ Vintage _____

Source _____ Price _____

Where tasted _____ Date _____

Occasion _____

With whom _____

Meal _____

Appearance _____ Bouquet _____

Balance _____ Taste _____

Body _____ Rating _____

Notes and comments _____

_____

_____

_____

_____

_____

Attach Label Here

Wine _____ Vintage _____

Source _____ Price _____

Where tasted _____ Date _____

Occasion _____

With whom _____

Meal _____

Appearance _____ Bouquet _____

Balance _____ Taste _____

Body _____ Rating _____

Notes and comments _____

_____

_____

_____

_____

Attach Label Here

Wine _____ Vintage _____

Source _____ Price _____

Where tasted _____ Date _____

Occasion _____

With whom _____

Meal _____

Appearance _____ Bouquet _____

Balance _____ Taste _____

Body _____ Rating _____

Notes and comments _____

_____

_____

_____

_____

Attach Label Here

Wine _____ Vintage _____

Source_____ Price _____

Where tasted_____ Date _____

Occasion _____

With whom _____

Meal _____

Appearance _____ Bouquet _____

Balance _____ Taste _____

Body _____ Rating _____

Notes and comments_____

_____

_____

_____

_____

Attach Label Here

Wine _____ Vintage _____

Source _____ Price _____

Where tasted _____ Date _____

Occasion _____

With whom _____

Meal _____

Appearance _____ Bouquet _____

Balance _____ Taste _____

Body _____ Rating _____

Notes and comments _____

_____

_____

_____

_____

Attach Label Here

Wine _____ Vintage _____

Source _____ Price _____

Where tasted _____ Date _____

Occasion _____

With whom _____

Meal _____

Appearance _____ Bouquet _____

Balance _____ Taste _____

Body _____ Rating _____

Notes and comments _____

_____

_____

_____

_____

Attach Label Here

Wine _____ Vintage _____

Source _____ Price _____

Where tasted _____ Date _____

Occasion _____

With whom _____

Meal _____

Appearance _____ Bouquet _____

Balance _____ Taste _____

Body _____ Rating _____

Notes and comments _____

_____

_____

_____

_____

Attach Label Here

Wine _____   Vintage _____

Source _____   Price _____

Where tasted _____   Date _____

Occasion _____

With whom _____

Meal _____

Appearance _____   Bouquet _____

Balance _____   Taste _____

Body _____   Rating _____

Notes and comments _____

_____

_____

_____

_____

Attach Label Here

Wine _____ Vintage _____

Source _____ Price _____

Where tasted _____ Date _____

Occasion _____

With whom _____

Meal _____

Appearance _____ Bouquet _____

Balance _____ Taste _____

Body _____ Rating _____

Notes and comments _____

_____

_____

_____

_____

Attach Label Here

Wine _____ Vintage _____

Source _____ Price _____

Where tasted _____ Date _____

Occasion _____

With whom _____

Meal _____

Appearance _____ Bouquet _____

Balance _____ Taste _____

Body _____ Rating _____

Notes and comments _____

_____

_____

_____

_____

Attach Label Here

Wine _____ Vintage _____

Source _____ Price _____

Where tasted _____ Date _____

Occasion _____

With whom _____

Meal _____

Appearance _____ Bouquet _____

Balance _____ Taste _____

Body _____ Rating _____

Notes and comments _____

_____

_____

_____

_____

Attach Label Here

Wine _____ Vintage _____

Source _____ Price _____

Where tasted _____ Date _____

Occasion _____

With whom _____

Meal _____

Appearance _____ Bouquet _____

Balance _____ Taste _____

Body _____ Rating _____

Notes and comments _____

_____

_____

_____

_____

Attach Label Here

Wine _____	Vintage _____
Source _____	Price _____
Where tasted _____	Date _____
Occasion _____	
With whom _____	
Meal _____	
Appearance _____	Bouquet _____
Balance _____	Taste _____
Body _____	Rating _____
Notes and comments _____	

_____

_____

_____

_____

Attach Label Here

Wine _____ Vintage _____

Source _____ Price _____

Where tasted _____ Date _____

Occasion _____

With whom _____

Meal _____

Appearance _____ Bouquet _____

Balance _____ Taste _____

Body _____ Rating _____

Notes and comments _____

_____

_____

_____

_____

Attach Label Here

Wine _____ Vintage _____

Source _____ Price _____

Where tasted _____ Date _____

Occasion _____

With whom _____

Meal _____

Appearance _____ Bouquet _____

Balance _____ Taste _____

Body _____ Rating _____

Notes and comments _____

_____ _____

_____

_____

_____

Attach Label Here

Wine _____ Vintage _____

Source _____ Price _____

Where tasted _____ Date _____

Occasion _____

With whom _____

Meal _____

Appearance _____ Bouquet _____

Balance _____ Taste _____

Body _____ Rating _____

Notes and comments _____

_____

_____

_____

_____

Attach Label Here

Wine _____ Vintage _____
Source _____ Price _____
Where tasted _____ Date _____
Occasion _____
With whom _____
Meal _____
Appearance _____ Bouquet _____
Balance _____ Taste _____
Body _____ Rating _____
Notes and comments _____
_____
_____
_____
_____

Attach Label Here

Wine _____ Vintage _____

Source _____ Price _____

Where tasted _____ Date _____

Occasion _____

With whom _____

Meal _____

Appearance _____ Bouquet _____

Balance _____ Taste _____

Body _____ Rating _____

Notes and comments _____

_____

_____

_____

_____

_____

Attach Label Here

Wine _____ Vintage _____

Source _____ Price _____

Where tasted _____ Date _____

Occasion _____

With whom _____

Meal _____

Appearance _____ Bouquet _____

Balance _____ Taste _____

Body _____ Rating _____

Notes and comments _____

_____

_____

_____

_____

Attach Label Here

Wine _____ Vintage _____

Source _____ Price _____

Where tasted _____ Date _____

Occasion _____

With whom _____

Meal _____

Appearance _____ Bouquet _____

Balance _____ Taste _____

Body _____ Rating _____

Notes and comments _____

_____

_____

_____

_____

Attach Label Here

Wine _____ Vintage _____

Source _____ Price _____

Where tasted _____ Date _____

Occasion _____

With whom _____

Meal _____

Appearance _____ Bouquet _____

Balance _____ Taste _____

Body _____ Rating _____

Notes and comments _____

_____

_____

_____

_____

Attach Label Here

Wine _____ Vintage _____

Source _____ Price _____

Where tasted_____ Date _____

Occasion _____

With whom _____

Meal _____

Appearance _____ Bouquet _____

Balance _____ Taste _____

Body _____ Rating _____

Notes and comments_____

_____

_____

_____

_____

Attach Label Here

Wine _____ Vintage _____

Source_____ Price _____

Where tasted_____ Date _____

Occasion _____

With whom _____

Meal _____

Appearance _____ Bouquet _____

Balance _____ Taste _____

Body _____ Rating _____

Notes and comments_____

_____

_____

_____

_____

Attach Label Here

Wine _____ Vintage _____

Source _____ Price _____

Where tasted _____ Date _____

Occasion _____

With whom _____

Meal _____

Appearance _____ Bouquet _____

Balance _____ Taste _____

Body _____ Rating _____

Notes and comments _____

_____

_____

_____

_____

Attach Label Here

Wine _____ Vintage _____

Source _____ Price _____

Where tasted _____ Date _____

Occasion _____

With whom _____

Meal _____

Appearance _____ Bouquet _____

Balance _____ Taste _____

Body _____ Rating _____

Notes and comments _____

_____

_____

_____

_____

Attach Label Here

Wine _____ Vintage _____

Source _____ Price _____

Where tasted _____ Date _____

Occasion _____

With whom _____

Meal _____

Appearance _____ Bouquet _____

Balance _____ Taste _____

Body _____ Rating _____

Notes and comments _____

_____

_____

_____

_____

Attach Label Here

Wine _____ Vintage _____

Source _____ Price _____

Where tasted _____ Date _____

Occasion _____

With whom _____

Meal _____

Appearance _____ Bouquet _____

Balance _____ Taste _____

Body _____ Rating _____

Notes and comments _____

_____

_____

_____

_____

Attach Label Here

Wine _____ Vintage _____

Source _____ Price _____

Where tasted _____ Date _____

Occasion _____

With whom _____

Meal _____

Appearance _____ Bouquet _____

Balance _____ Taste _____

Body _____ Rating _____

Notes and comments _____

_____

_____

_____

_____

Attach Label Here

Wine _____ Vintage _____

Source _____ Price _____

Where tasted _____ Date _____

Occasion _____

With whom _____

Meal _____

Appearance _____ Bouquet _____

Balance _____ Taste _____

Body _____ Rating _____

Notes and comments _____

_____

_____

_____

_____

Attach Label Here

Wine _____	Vintage _____
Source _____	Price _____
Where tasted _____	Date _____
Occasion _____	
With whom _____	
Meal _____	
Appearance _____	Bouquet _____
Balance _____	Taste _____
Body _____	Rating _____
Notes and comments _____	

_____

_____

_____

_____

Attach Label Here

Wine _____ Vintage _____

Source _____ Price _____

Where tasted _____ Date _____

Occasion _____

With whom _____

Meal _____

Appearance _____ Bouquet _____

Balance _____ Taste _____

Body _____ Rating _____

Notes and comments _____

_____

_____

_____

_____

Attach Label Here

Wine _____ Vintage _____

Source _____ Price _____

Where tasted _____ Date _____

Occasion _____

With whom _____

Meal _____

Appearance _____ Bouquet _____

Balance _____ Taste _____

Body _____ Rating _____

Notes and comments _____

_____

_____

_____

_____

Attach Label Here

Wine _____ Vintage _____

Source _____ Price _____

Where tasted _____ Date _____

Occasion _____

With whom _____

Meal _____

Appearance _____ Bouquet _____

Balance _____ Taste _____

Body _____ Rating _____

Notes and comments _____

_____

_____

_____

_____

Attach Label Here

Wine _____ Vintage _____

Source _____ Price _____

Where tasted _____ Date _____

Occasion _____

With whom _____

Meal _____

Appearance _____ Bouquet _____

Balance _____ Taste _____

Body _____ Rating _____

Notes and comments _____

_____

_____

_____

_____

Attach Label Here

Wine _____ Vintage _____

Source _____ Price _____

Where tasted _____ Date _____

Occasion _____

With whom _____

Meal _____

Appearance _____ Bouquet _____

Balance _____ Taste _____

Body _____ Rating _____

Notes and comments _____
_____
_____
_____
_____
_____

Attach Label Here

Wine _____   Vintage _____

Source _____   Price _____

Where tasted _____   Date _____

Occasion _____

With whom _____

Meal _____

Appearance _____   Bouquet _____

Balance _____   Taste _____

Body _____   Rating _____

Notes and comments _____

_____

_____

_____

_____

Attach Label Here

Wine _____ Vintage _____

Source _____ Price _____

Where tasted _____ Date _____

Occasion _____

With whom _____

Meal _____

Appearance _____ Bouquet _____

Balance _____ Taste _____

Body _____ Rating _____

Notes and comments _____

_____

_____

_____

_____

Attach Label Here

Wine _____   Vintage _____

Source _____   Price _____

Where tasted _____   Date _____

Occasion _____

With whom _____

Meal _____

Appearance _____   Bouquet _____

Balance _____   Taste _____

Body _____   Rating _____

Notes and comments _____

_____

_____

_____

_____

Attach Label Here

Wine _____ Vintage _____

Source _____ Price _____

Where tasted _____ Date _____

Occasion _____

With whom _____

Meal _____

Appearance _____ Bouquet _____

Balance _____ Taste _____

Body _____ Rating _____

Notes and comments _____

_____

_____

_____

_____

Attach Label Here

Wine _____ Vintage _____

Source _____ Price _____

Where tasted _____ Date _____

Occasion _____

With whom _____

Meal _____

Appearance _____ Bouquet _____

Balance _____ Taste _____

Body _____ Rating _____

Notes and comments _____

_____

_____

_____

_____

Attach Label Here

Wine _____ Vintage _____

Source _____ Price _____

Where tasted _____ Date _____

Occasion _____

With whom _____

Meal _____

Appearance _____ Bouquet _____

Balance _____ Taste _____

Body _____ Rating _____

Notes and comments _____

_____

_____

_____

_____

Attach Label Here

Wine _____ Vintage _____

Source _____ Price _____

Where tasted _____ Date _____

Occasion _____

With whom _____

Meal _____

Appearance _____ Bouquet _____

Balance _____ Taste _____

Body _____ Rating _____

Notes and comments _____

_____

_____

_____

_____

Attach Label Here

Wine _____   Vintage _____

Source _____   Price _____

Where tasted _____   Date _____

Occasion _____

With whom _____

Meal _____

Appearance _____   Bouquet _____

Balance _____   Taste _____

Body _____   Rating _____

Notes and comments _____

_____

_____

_____

_____

Attach Label Here

Wine _____ Vintage _____

Source _____ Price _____

Where tasted _____ Date _____

Occasion _____

With whom _____

Meal _____

Appearance _____ Bouquet _____

Balance _____ Taste _____

Body _____ Rating _____

Notes and comments _____

_____

_____

_____

_____

Attach Label Here

Wine _____ Vintage _____

Source _____ Price _____

Where tasted _____ Date _____

Occasion _____

With whom _____

Meal _____

Appearance _____ Bouquet _____

Balance _____ Taste _____

Body _____ Rating _____

Notes and comments _____

_____

_____

_____

_____

Attach Label Here

Wine _____   Vintage _____

Source _____   Price _____

Where tasted _____   Date _____

Occasion _____

With whom _____

Meal _____

Appearance _____   Bouquet _____

Balance _____   Taste _____

Body _____   Rating _____

Notes and comments _____

_____

_____

_____

_____

_____

Attach Label Here

Wine _____ Vintage _____

Source _____ Price _____

Where tasted _____ Date _____

Occasion _____

With whom _____

Meal _____

Appearance _____ Bouquet _____

Balance _____ Taste _____

Body _____ Rating _____

Notes and comments _____

_____

_____

_____

_____

Attach Label Here

Wine _____ Vintage _____

Source _____ Price _____

Where tasted _____ Date _____

Occasion _____

With whom _____

Meal _____

Appearance _____ Bouquet _____

Balance _____ Taste _____

Body _____ Rating _____

Notes and comments _____

_____

_____

_____

_____

Attach Label Here

Wine _____ Vintage _____

Source _____ Price _____

Where tasted _____ Date _____

Occasion _____

With whom _____

Meal _____

Appearance _____ Bouquet _____

Balance _____ Taste _____

Body _____ Rating _____

Notes and comments _____

_____

_____

_____

_____

Attach Label Here

Wine _____ Vintage _____

Source _____ Price _____

Where tasted _____ Date _____

Occasion _____

With whom _____

Meal _____

Appearance _____ Bouquet _____

Balance _____ Taste _____

Body _____ Rating _____

Notes and comments _____

_____

_____

_____

_____

Attach Label Here

Wine _____ Vintage _____

Source _____ Price _____

Where tasted _____ Date _____

Occasion _____

With whom _____

Meal _____

Appearance _____ Bouquet _____

Balance _____ Taste _____

Body _____ Rating _____

Notes and comments _____

_____

_____

_____

_____

_____

Attach Label Here

Wine _____ Vintage _____

Source _____ Price _____

Where tasted _____ Date _____

Occasion _____

With whom _____

Meal _____

Appearance _____ Bouquet _____

Balance _____ Taste _____

Body _____ Rating _____

Notes and comments _____

_____

_____

_____

_____

Attach Label Here

Wine _____ Vintage _____
Source _____ Price _____
Where tasted _____ Date _____
Occasion _____
With whom _____
Meal _____
Appearance _____ Bouquet _____
Balance _____ Taste _____
Body _____ Rating _____
Notes and comments _____
_____
_____
_____
_____

Attach Label Here

Wine _____ Vintage _____

Source_____ Price _____

Where tasted_____ Date _____

Occasion _____

With whom _____

Meal _____

Appearance _____ Bouquet _____

Balance _____ Taste _____

Body _____ Rating _____

Notes and comments_____

_____

_____

_____

_____

Attach Label Here

Wine _____ Vintage _____

Source _____ Price _____

Where tasted _____ Date _____

Occasion _____

With whom _____

Meal _____

Appearance _____ Bouquet _____

Balance _____ Taste _____

Body _____ Rating _____

Notes and comments _____

_____

_____

_____

_____

Attach Label Here

Wine _____   Vintage _____

Source _____   Price _____

Where tasted _____   Date _____

Occasion _____

With whom _____

Meal _____

Appearance _____   Bouquet _____

Balance _____   Taste _____

Body _____   Rating _____

Notes and comments _____

_____

_____

_____

_____

Attach Label Here

Wine _____ Vintage _____

Source _____ Price _____

Where tasted _____ Date _____

Occasion _____

With whom _____

Meal _____

Appearance _____ Bouquet _____

Balance _____ Taste _____

Body _____ Rating _____

Notes and comments _____

_____

_____

_____

_____

Attach Label Here

Wine _____   Vintage _____

Source _____   Price _____

Where tasted _____   Date _____

Occasion _____

With whom _____

Meal _____

Appearance _____   Bouquet _____

Balance _____   Taste _____

Body _____   Rating _____

Notes and comments _____

_____

_____

_____

_____

Attach Label Here

Wine _____ Vintage _____

Source _____ Price _____

Where tasted _____ Date _____

Occasion _____

With whom _____

Meal _____

Appearance _____ Bouquet _____

Balance _____ Taste _____

Body _____ Rating _____

Notes and comments _____

_____

_____

_____

_____

Attach Label Here

Wine _____ Vintage _____

Source _____ Price _____

Where tasted _____ Date _____

Occasion _____

With whom _____

Meal _____

Appearance _____ Bouquet _____

Balance _____ Taste _____

Body _____ Rating _____

Notes and comments _____

_____

_____

_____

_____

Attach Label Here

Wine _____   Vintage _____

Source _____   Price _____

Where tasted _____   Date _____

Occasion _____

With whom _____

Meal _____

Appearance _____   Bouquet _____

Balance _____   Taste _____

Body _____   Rating _____

Notes and comments _____

_____

_____

_____

_____

Attach Label Here

Wine _____ Vintage _____

Source _____ Price _____

Where tasted _____ Date _____

Occasion _____

With whom _____

Meal _____

Appearance _____ Bouquet _____

Balance _____ Taste _____

Body _____ Rating _____

Notes and comments _____

_____

_____

_____

_____

Attach Label Here

Wine _____   Vintage _____

Source _____   Price _____

Where tasted _____   Date _____

Occasion _____

With whom _____

Meal _____

Appearance _____   Bouquet _____

Balance _____   Taste _____

Body _____   Rating _____

Notes and comments _____

_____

_____

_____

_____

_____

Attach Label Here

Wine _____ Vintage _____

Source _____ Price _____

Where tasted _____ Date _____

Occasion _____

With whom _____

Meal _____

Appearance _____ Bouquet _____

Balance _____ Taste _____

Body _____ Rating _____

Notes and comments _____

_____

_____

_____

_____

Attach Label Here

Wine _____ Vintage _____

Source _____ Price _____

Where tasted _____ Date _____

Occasion _____

With whom _____

Meal _____

Appearance _____ Bouquet _____

Balance _____ Taste _____

Body _____ Rating _____

Notes and comments _____

_____

_____

_____

_____

Attach Label Here

Wine _____ Vintage _____

Source _____ Price _____

Where tasted _____ Date _____

Occasion _____

With whom _____

Meal _____

Appearance _____ Bouquet _____

Balance _____ Taste _____

Body _____ Rating _____

Notes and comments _____

_____

_____

_____

_____

Attach Label Here

Wine _____ Vintage _____

Source _____ Price _____

Where tasted _____ Date _____

Occasion _____

With whom _____

Meal _____

Appearance _____ Bouquet _____

Balance _____ Taste _____

Body _____ Rating _____

Notes and comments _____

_____

_____

_____

_____

_____

Attach Label Here

Wine _____	Vintage _____
Source _____	Price _____
Where tasted _____	Date _____
Occasion _____	
With whom _____	
Meal _____	
Appearance _____	Bouquet _____
Balance _____	Taste _____
Body _____	Rating _____

Notes and comments _____
_____
_____
_____
_____
_____

Attach Label Here

Wine _____ Vintage _____

Source _____ Price _____

Where tasted _____ Date _____

Occasion _____

With whom _____

Meal _____

Appearance _____ Bouquet _____

Balance _____ Taste _____

Body _____ Rating _____

Notes and comments _____

_____

_____

_____

_____

FAVORITE WINES

Wine	Vintage	Rating

DIRECTORY OF WINE MERCHANTS

Merchant	Phone #	Contact

NOTES

NOTES

NOTES

NOTES

NOTES

NOTES